SATISFYING PATTERNS

COLORING BOOK

BELONGS TO:

____

We Hope That You Love
This Book And
Enjoy Every Single Pages

RELAXING

INSPIRING

CREATIVE

ENJOYABLE

If You Like This Book Please
Give Us Your Honest
Feedback On Amazon

It's Really Helpful For Us

Made in the USA
Las Vegas, NV
14 June 2025

23648468R00057